UNITED KINGDUMB

D1235906

OTHER BOOKS BY LELAND GREGORY

UNITED KINGDUMB

Idiots from the British Isles

Leland Gregory

**Andrews McMeel
Publishing, LLC**

Kansas City • Sydney • London

10 11 12 13 14 RR2 10 9 8 7 6 5 4 3 2 1

ISBN-13: 978-0-7407-9743-9
ISBN-10: 0-7407-9743-3

Library of Congress Control Number: 2010921946

www.andrewsmcmeel.com

Attention: Schools and Businesses
Andrews McMeel books are available at quantity discounts with bulk purchase for educational, business, or sales promotional use. For information, please write to: Special Sales Department, Andrews McMeel Publishing, LLC, 1130 Walnut Street, Kansas City, Missouri 64106.

UNITED KINGDUMB

Big Mac Attack

In order to keep the general public from becoming confused about who's who, companies are allowed to trademark their names so other companies can't use them. One of the most diligent protectors of name identification is McDonald's. They've gone after mom-and-pop companies, medium-size companies, and even companies owned by people named McDonald—and won.

But McDonald's suffered a setback in the United Kingdom when London's High Court allowed Frank Yu Kwan Yuen's registration for "McChina" as a British trademark for his restaurant. "It appears to me on analysis that McDonald's are virtually seeking to monopolize all names and words with the prefix Mc or Mac," Judge David Neuberger ruled, adding that there was an "absence of any evidence of confusion" among the general population from the Chinese restaurant's name.

After hearing the court's ruling, Yuen said he was "as happy as a drunken prawn"—an item, I hope, that doesn't appear on McChina's menu.

I Thought They
Were Shy

British scientists were honored with the 2002 Ig Nobel Prize for
their research into the reproductive habits of the ostrich. Their
observations uncovered that ostriches become more sexually
aroused when there is a human present—in fact, some ostriches
tried to become amorous with the human observers.

Winston Churchill's mother, Jennie Jerome, was born
in America in Brooklyn, New York.

Lay About

British workers were urged to bum around, stop working, and in effect do nothing in order to celebrate the second annual National Slacker Day. But the event wasn't as popular as most people would think. A poll conducted during that week showed that 59 percent of the people claimed they don't do much at work anyway, other than use company time to talk with friends and family and catch up on correspondence through company e-mail.

The special day of observance to observe doing nothing generated hardly any interest. People slacked off doing anything to celebrate National Slacker Day—making the event both a success and a failure.

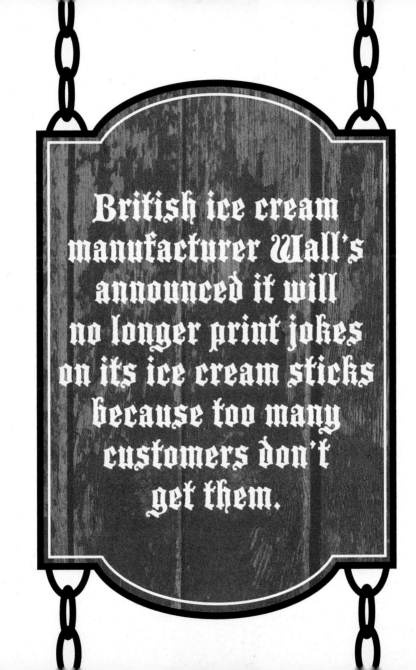

British ice cream manufacturer Wall's announced it will no longer print jokes on its ice cream sticks because too many customers don't get them.

Working Your Way Up from the Bottom

A "whistleblower" is someone who discovers and then reports illegal or unscrupulous activity in the workplace. One vigilant British worker, who obviously had some spare time on his hands—or intestinal problems—measured several rolls of toilet paper and found they had only 200 sheets as opposed to the 320 sheets stated in the contract with the supplier. His employer, West Somerset District Council, demanded the vendor wipe the slate clean and was awarded £17,150. For saving the company so much money, the employee was given only a few days off. So if the company is ever "rolled," you can be sure who did it.

Forgive Them for They Know Not What They Do

Some overzealous volunteers at a church at Newquay, Cardiganshire, were running a jumble sale to help raise money for the church. In order to get as much stuff as possible to sell at bargain prices, one of the volunteers accidentally snatched the church's collection of gold and silver items (valued at £9,150) along with some not-so-expensive bric-a-brac and sold the entire box for about £10! May the Lord be with him.

In 1700s England it was possible to buy insurance against going to hell.

Two In, Three Out

We've all seen movies where prisoners secretly exchange things through the bars of their cells. But one couple in the Swansea Crown Court Building in South Wales passed something through the bars that you would see only in a different kind of movie.

An investigation was launched when an inmate, Donna Stokes, became pregnant after having sex with her boyfriend through the bars of their respective holding cells. Both were awaiting a hearing on burglary and theft charges and were in adjoining temporary cells and, as Stokes said, "We hadn't seen each other for months." Sounds like a lot more fun than rattling a tin cup against the bars, doesn't it?

The Bump and Grind

John Turner of Thornaby-on-Tees sought and was granted a divorce from his wife, Pauline, on the grounds of unreasonable behavior. The man couldn't stand his wife's compulsive habit of rearranging the furniture every day of their thirty-eight-year marriage.

The first general income tax ever was implemented in Great Britain by William Pitt the Younger in his budget of December 1798 to finance the Napoleonic Wars. The tax was imposed at a rate of 10 percent on all incomes exceeding £200; income under £60 was exempt. After the war, the tax was repealed but then put into place again in 1842 by then prime minister Sir Robert Peel.

May I Have the Envelope, Please?

In a February 2002 survey in Great Britain, one in nine people admitted to sending themselves Valentine's Day cards so that they would receive at least one. Of the remaining respondents, one out of every three had received a card from their own children and one in ten had stolen them from someone else in the house.

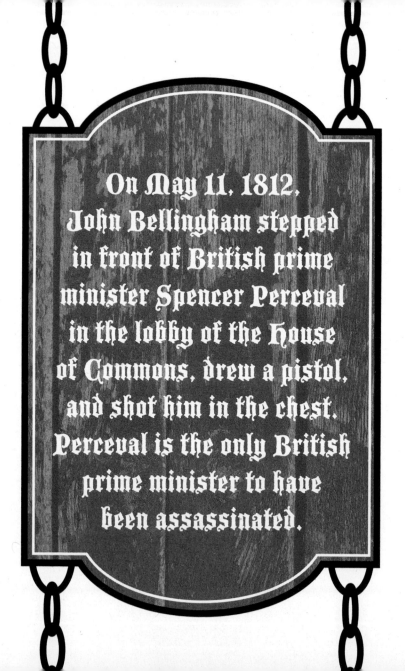

In a Class by Itself

In 1917, during the height of World War I, the Germans announced unrestricted submarine warfare (sinking merchant ships without warning) in an attempt to cut off trade and supplies to Britain. The British Admiralty produced their answer to the German U-boats: a fleet of 325-foot-long steam-powered submarines called "K-class submarines." They were soon nicknamed "Kalamity class"; here's why:

❉ K1 collided with K4 off the Danish coast on November 18, 1917, and was purposely sunk to avoid capture.

❉ K2 caught fire on its maiden dive.

❉ K3 sank for no apparent reason (with the Prince of Wales aboard) and then mysteriously surfaced again.

❉ K5 was lost due to unknown reasons during a mock battle in the Bay of Biscay on January 20, 1921. The submarine signaled she was diving and nothing was ever heard from her again.

❉ K13 sank on January 19, 1917, during sea trials when an intake failed to close while she was submerging and her engine room flooded. She was eventually salvaged and recommissioned as K22 in March 1917.

Only one K boat ever engaged an enemy vessel, hitting a German U-boat with a torpedo, which failed to explode. In 1918 (after the accidental deaths of some 250 British sailors), the K project was abandoned.

Sub-Story

Two K-class boats were lost in an incident known as the "Battle of May Island" on January 31, 1918. The cruiser HMS *Fearless* collided with the lead submarine, K17, which sank in about eight minutes. In an attempt to get out of the cruiser's way, K4 was struck by K6, nearly cutting her in half, and was then struck by K7. She sank with all her crew. At the same time, K22 (the recommissioned K13) and K14 collided, although both survived. In a little over an hour and fifteen minutes, two submarines had been sunk, four were badly damaged, and 105 crewmembers were killed.

Really Up a Tree

In 1978, the British army was called in to serve as temporary firemen during a strike of local firefighters. An elderly woman called the firehouse on January 14 to ask for assistance as her cat had climbed a tree and was unable to get down. The army arrived quickly and valiantly rescued the woman's cat, placing the purring puss into the woman's grateful hands.

So happy was the woman with the army's handling of the situation that she invited the brave men in for tea. They accepted her invitation, and after a pleasant time together the army volunteers/firemen bade their host a fond farewell, got back into their fire trucks, and promptly ran over and killed the rescued cat.

Pie in the Sky

When a jilted boyfriend wants revenge there's no telling what he might do—and in the case of Liam McGarry of Scotland there was no telling why he did what he did; in fact, he didn't even know.

McGarry turned up at the home of Laura Barr, who had broken off their relationship a month earlier. She later said McGarry didn't even look like himself—mainly because he was covered in mincemeat. A neighbor came over to help remove McGarry after he had slapped Barr and spat chunks of meat in her face. In a March 13, 2004, article in the *Daily Record,* McGarry's defense lawyer was quoted as saying, "He is at a complete loss to explain the significance of the mince or why he had coated himself in it."

Dead on Target

In 1943, Great Britain was crafting a plan to invade Sicily. Needing the Germans and Italians to think they were invading elsewhere, they hired a spy. He had to be stiff—and I don't mean uptight. I mean an honest-to-goodness dead person.

They gave the dead man a new name, Major William Martin, some fictitious history, some English currency, a few love letters, and a cryptic letter outlining an imminent invasion of either Sardinia, on the west side of Italy, or Greece, on the east. The body was tossed from a British submarine off the coast of Spain, where it soon washed ashore.

The Germans believed the information was correct and moved troops to the coasts of Greece and Sardinia. That night, thousands of British soldiers parachuted into the relatively unguarded island of Sicily. They are credited with being the crucial first line of soldiers that ultimately made the D-Day invasion possible. A fictitious dead man played a key role in one of the most decisive battles of World War II—I guess that's truly esprit d'corpse.

Green Jelly Genes

Since discovering that certain jellyfish have genes that make them glow green, scientists have been tinkering with ways to use that unique phenomenon in other plants and animals. The Scottish Agricultural College in June 1999 created a potato that glows green when it needs water. And the University of Hertfordshire announced in October 1999 that it would genetically alter Douglas spruce trees with jellyfish genes in order to create naturally illuminating Christmas trees.

Don't Quit Your Day Job

While studying law at St. John's College, Oxford, during the early 1970s, future UK prime minister Tony Blair was in a rock band called Ugly Rumours. The band's name was taken from the album cover for *Grateful Dead from the Mars Hotel*. The words "Ugly Rumors" appear upside down and backward on the cover. Blair sang and played guitar in the band.

When Britain
abandoned the
Julian calendar
and adopted the
Gregorian calendar
on Wednesday,
September 2, 1752,
the next day
was Thursday,
September 14, 1752.

I've Heard of Ham-Fisted Before But . . .

The *Daily Mail* reported in April 2000 that Esporta Health Clubs had designed a new line of socks to help people lose weight. Named "FatSox," these revolutionary socks, which were said to employ the patented nylon polymer FloraAstraTetrazine, reportedly sucked "excess lipids from the body through the sweat." Once "FatSox" were soaked with perspiration, said the inventor, Professor Frank Ellis Elgood, the wearer would simply remove the socks and wash them—removing dirt, grime, smell, and, most important, fat.

The article was reported through worldwide media outlets. The editors who believed this April Fool's story should wear "FatSox" instead of hats to decrease the size of their fat heads.

Cutting Off Your Circulation

Unhappy with the depth of reporting in English newspapers, Lionel Burleigh decided to publish his own paper in 1965 called the *Commonwealth Sentinel*. Burleigh worked diligently for weeks writing articles, promoting the newspaper on billboards, selling advertising space, and printing fifty thousand copies to make the first edition a success.

On February 6, 1965, after the newspaper had left the printers, an exhausted Burleigh was resting in his hotel room when he was interrupted by a call from the London constabulary. "Have you anything to do with the *Commonwealth Sentinel*?" the officer asked. "Because there are fifty thousand on the outside entrance to Brown's Hotel and they're blocking Albemarle Street." While attending to the hundreds of details needed when publishing a newspaper, Burleigh had forgotten one: He never got a distributor. Britain's "most fearless paper" folded the following day.

Testing One, Two . . .

On August 3, 1970, a sixty-two-year-old woman, Miriam Hargrave, of Yorkshire, finally passed her driving test . . . on her fortieth attempt. After so much struggle and perseverance one would assume she started driving right away. But, unfortunately, after spending so much money on driving lessons—£440—she couldn't afford to buy a car. If it took her forty attempts to pass a simple driving test it's a good thing she never got on the road.

*No reigning British monarch ever visited Canada or
the United States until George VI in 1939.*

Bouncing Baby Burglar

"It's the only area children have got to play in," complains Matthew Nice of Wicklow, Essex, concerning the London and Quadrant Housing Association's demand that he remove a three-foot toy trampoline from the social housing unit's yard. According to a July 1, 2009, article in the *Telegraph,* the association's fear isn't for the safety of the children; it's because they believe the trampoline could be used by burglars to bounce into open upstairs windows.

Although Nice has voiced his opinion about the intelligence level of a burglar who would try to use a child's trampoline to spring through a window, the association isn't budging. "The housing association is not making any allowances, and this is just taking things too far," he complained.

Get a Tan by Standing in the English Rain

In many Mediterranean countries solar-powered city parking meters are used, saving a fortune in maintenance costs. So city officials in Nottingham decided to get in on the action and spent more than £1 million installing solar-powered parking meters on their city streets. There is one glaring problem—or should I say a problem that isn't glaring—the sun. Mediterranean countries get a lot of sun and, even in the summer, England doesn't. As of August 2001, more than 245 of the parking meters were out of commission, allowing hundreds of motorists to park for free.

The Anglo-Zanzibar War was fought between the United Kingdom and Zanzibar on August 27, 1896. It was the shortest war in history, lasting only thirty-eight minutes.

A Fork in the Family Tree

A man from Lancashire, Ian Lewis, spent three decades tracing his family's roots back to the seventeenth century. Lewis traveled extensively in England interviewing some two thousand relatives to map out his genealogy, and he learned something he didn't know: He was adopted. It turns out his real name isn't Lewis at all, but David Thornton. His parents adopted him when he was one month old. Lewis/Thornton said he will start tracing his new identity immediately after he roots out why his parents never told him he was adopted.

Runaway Bride

While looking over the marriage announcements in her local newspaper, a London woman saw something she recognized. It wasn't a person—it was a dress. The woman identified a dress that had been stolen from her shop over four months before. Having the full name of both the intended bride and the groom, the woman reported the incident to the police.

"I was amazed that she had the cheek to let her picture be published in the paper wearing a dress stolen under my very nose," said the original dress's owner. The bride-to-be almost became a prisoner-to-be but was only fined £185 after she confessed to handling stolen property. If she were arrested, I wonder if the other prisoners would have chanted, "Here comes the bride. Here comes the bride."

A Token of Their Appreciation

In October 1971, the Arbeia Roman Fort and Museum in South Shields was proudly displaying an exhibition of Roman artifacts found nearby (the museum is located near the end of Hadrian's Wall, which was built by the Romans around AD 160). One case contained a Roman sestertius coin identified by museum experts as having been minted sometime between AD 135 and AD 138.

But one visitor, nine-year-old Fiona Gordon, claimed to have seen similar coins much later than that given out as tokens by a local soda bottler. She pointed out the soda bottler's trademark on the coin. The "R" that museum officials had originally taken to mean "Roman" actually stood for the soft drink manufacturer Robinson's. The realization they had been displaying a fake Roman coin made the curators feel like a gluteus maximus.

A Cramped Expression

Some common phrases that we take for granted don't make a lot of sense unless you know the context in which they were created. One example is the phrase "charley horse." We know what a charley horse is; it's a muscle cramp. But how did it get such a weird name?

In 1640, Charles I of England expanded the London police force. The nickname "Charley" was given to new recruits in mock honor of the person responsible for their hiring, Charles I. The new recruits soon discovered there wasn't enough money to supply them with horses, so they were forced to patrol on foot. After a full day of walking the beat the new officers joked that their sore feet and legs were the result of riding "Charley's horse."

I'm Going to Go to Disney World

Roy Dennis of Hampshire was visiting his son Edward in Auckland, New Zealand, in October 2002 on what he had anticipated as being a vacation of a lifetime. He'll definitely remember it for a lifetime because he wound up in the hospital three times in two days.

First, Dennis had to undergo emergency surgery and was confined to a wheelchair after he snapped an ankle while skydiving. Then he was bitten by a puffer fish, the most poisonous animal in the world next to the golden poison frog, and needed a tetanus shot. The next day Dennis went to an adventure park where staff put the sixty-year-old man in his wheelchair in a special car for the tour. But the chair wasn't secured, and Dennis spun out of the car and into a window, breaking his nose.

You Say Tomato and I Say Tomato

Raeoul Sebastian and Emma Nunn, both nineteen, of London, purchased airline tickets to Sydney for a three-week vacation, and they got just want they asked for. They were planning on staying in Sydney, Australia, but they actually wound up in Sydney, Nova Scotia, in August 2002.

Even though Australia is a commonwealth of England, the couple didn't realize they were headed north instead of south until they had a plane changeover in Halifax, Nova Scotia, after a six-hour flight from England. The confused couple decided to stay in Sydney, Nova Scotia, for a few days and then save their money for a real trip to Sydney, Australia, the following year.

Although portrayed as a hunchback in *Richard III* by William Shakespeare, the real Richard III wasn't a hunchback; in fact, his contemporaries considered him handsome. It's also unlikely that he murdered his brother George as the Shakespearean play proposes.

Over and Under

According to a Reuters article from January 28, 2002, an overweight man who fell asleep on a passenger train heading to Manchester slid out of his seat, became wedged under a table, and couldn't get out. Firefighters struggled for forty-five minutes before finally freeing the portly passenger.

A July 11, 2002, *Daily Telegraph* article told the story of a seventeen-year-old woman who had just arrived back in England from Dubai. She was detained when airport agents noticed that the faux chameleon pattern on her hat was, in fact, an endangered—and very much alive—real chameleon.

Stone-Cold Suspect

A tourist traveling by train through Skegness, Lincolnshire, in July 2001 thought she had spotted a real local attraction and called police to complain about a dancing naked man with long hair and a beard. It didn't take authorities long to realize that the woman was talking about a statue of the town's mascot, the "Jolly Fisherman."

Inspector Paul Elliot reported that some of his men were "amused" at the mistaken identity but that the "woman made the call in good faith and we responded as we always do." I guess that means this had happened before.

Boys and Their Toys

When Carol Dukes discovered that her eleven-year-old son, Charlie, had left his Game Boy behind when he went to camp she decided to take it to him. She left her home in Berkshire in September 2001 and traveled by plane, taxis, and a ferry to find him on the isolated island of Iona, Scotland.

"If you decide to do something you do it and worry about the money later," Dukes said. "But I think everyone was quite surprised to see me." They weren't so surprised to see Dukes, but they were surprised to see the Game Boy; Charlie was attending camp "to learn about life without modern amenities."

Colin Braggs was arrested while trying to break into a police car in Frome, Somerset. Being that the windows were misted, Braggs hadn't noticed the two policemen sitting inside the car.

Bangers and Mash

John Hatfield, forty-six, was driving near his home in South Woodham Ferrers, in the borough of Chelmsford in Essex on a warm day with his window down when something flew in and hit him squarely on the nose. "He lost quite a lot of blood from his injury," said paramedic Dave Holton, who was called to the scene. "After we cleaned him he decided not to go to hospital, but he has been left with a very swollen nose."

According to an April 20, 2005, article in the *Guardian,* Hatfield was struck on the face with a sausage. The sausage tosser remains on the loose, and police said they are handling the case as an assault.

Urine Trouble Now!

Thieves in Coventry may have gotten pissed on piss. A van was broken into and crooks made off with two cases of wine and two cases of a bottled product called "Silent Roar." Since the wine and the other product were in the same van, the unsuspecting thieves might have thought "Silent Roar" is some kind of powerful alcohol. "If they don't know what 'Silent Roar' is, they might end up drinking the lot," said a police officer investigating the break-in.

The product is used to keep cats off gardens, and its main ingredient is lion's urine. If the crooks drank the stuff there would have been a roar, all right, but I don't think it would have been silent!

In Scotland it is illegal to be drunk and in possession of a cow.

A Lofty Lifter

In January 1997, Michael Coulter was seen shoplifting in a small store in Cookstown, Ireland. Coulter had lifted shoes, socks, and boxer shorts and was quickly and easily apprehended by police.

Even if he had worn a disguise he would have been readily spotted—at seven-foot-five, Coulter is reported to be the tallest man in Ireland. Remarked one officer, "Everyone knows him, and you can see him coming a mile away." Of course, everyone makes a mistake now and then—but this was a giant one.

Wide-Eyed Wonder

According to an article in the July 7, 2008, edition of the *Daily Mail,* Britain's Sea Life Centre announced a study to determine if octopuses use certain tentacles or random tentacles when faced with complex situations. In order to test their hypothesis, the aquarium planned to give the octopuses Rubik's Cube toys to play with.

"HUMAN CANNONBALL FIRED OVER HIS FEAR OF FLYING"

✿ *Times* headline, June 16, 2005 ✿

The Sacred Cow

In a February 2005 *Times* article, animal welfare professors at Britain's Bristol University explained that they were prepared to present research findings to the June conference on Compassion in World Farming. Their findings, they said, will show that cows experience emotions (fear and happiness), can form friendships, and are good at problem solving (brainwaves measured with electroencephalography showed peaks as a cow sought a path to food). They also discovered that cows can be moody and are capable of holding a grudge against other cows for months or even years.

The Deepest Cut

The *Independent* reported on September 30, 2003, about the cause of a delay in the Tube train in London's Underground. Apparently a trainee driver had pleaded with two colleagues to stop discussing the grisly details of a recent vasectomy operation. When they continued with their conversation, the trainee passed out and fell out of the cab.

The Bank of England was founded by a Scotsman,
Sir William Paterson, in 1694.

An Explosive Bill

The *Irish Independent* reported on June 27, 2008, that after languishing in the Irish legislature for two years, the Nuclear Test Ban Bill of 2006 had been dusted off and reexamined. The bill was originally drafted following the dictates of the U.N. Comprehensive Nuclear Test Ban Treaty, with provisions specific to Ireland. The original punishment set forth for those found guilty of detonating a nuclear weapon in Ireland was up to twelve months in jail and/ or a fine not to exceed €5,000. The proposed punishment in the amended bill is expected to be more congruous with the offense.

Egg-Cellent

Finally, science has tackled the age-old problem of when an egg has been properly boiled soft, medium, or hard. The *Times* reported on July 31, 2006, that the British Egg Information Service (I'm not joking) had announced the perfection and availability of the "smart egg." You can throw that old egg timer away: The new "smart egg" has an invisible ink on the shell that turns black at the moment of your boiled preference.

It's Not Just a Good Book—It's a Great Book!

In 1631, King Charles I ordered one thousand Bibles from an English printer named Robert Barker. Printing was not an exact science in those days, and sometimes mistakes were made and usually overlooked—but not in this case. Barker inadvertently left out a single word in the seventh commandment in Exodus 20:14—the word "not." Readers were shocked to find out that God had commanded Moses "Thou shalt commit adultery" as opposed to "Thou shalt not commit adultery."

King Charles I was not amused by this mistake and ordered all the Bibles destroyed, fined Barker £300 (a lifetime's wages in those days), and revoked his printing license—Barker was out of business. Not all the Bibles were destroyed; eleven are known to still exist. Because of the infamous mistake this printing of the official King James Version is referred to as "The Wicked Bible."

March of the Penguins

Numerous reports from the Royal Air Force during the 1982 Falklands War stated that penguins would become so mesmerized by watching airplanes fly overhead that they would fall over backward.

On February 2, 2001, BBC News reported that British scientists had conducted a five-week study into the pendulum penguin phenomenon and concluded that penguins don't, in fact, lose their balance and fall over backward while watching low-flying aircraft. Now we can all rest a little easier.

Andrew Bonar Law is usually forgotten for two simple reasons: One, he was the only British prime minister to have been born outside the British Isles (he was born in Canada), and, two, he was the shortest-serving prime minister of the twentieth century (serving only 211 days from October 23, 1922 to May 22, 1923). He is frequently referred to as "the unknown prime minister."

Coasting to Success

Ian Johnston, an aerodynamic expert at Britain's Open University, and Hazel Lucas, a graduate student in engineering at Oxford University, designed the ultimate beer coaster. "Pub mats" are often used in a popular drinking game called "Smash and Grab." According to a November 3, 2003, BBC News report, the two inventors designed a machine to simulate the act of flipping the coaster, and from their findings designed the king of coasters.

The Yanks Are Coming

Even though Nancy Witcher Astor was the first woman to serve as a member of Parliament in the British House of Commons from 1919 to 1945 (Constance Markiewicz of the Sinn Féin Party was elected in 1918 but did not take her seat), she was born in the United States in Danville, Virginia. Her second husband, Waldorf Astor, was elected in December 1910 as a Conservative member of Parliament for Plymouth and then in 1918 for Plymouth Sutton. He was born in New York City.

"The abdomen, the chest, and the brain will forever be shut from the intrusion of the wise and humane surgeon."

—Sir John Eric Ericksen, appointed surgeon-extraordinary
to Queen Victoria in 1873

I Hate It When That Happens

Police were called to Islington in North London to follow up on a report of a young man on fire. When police and fire crews arrived they discovered the youth in a front garden, engulfed in flames, and they quickly put the fire out. The seventeen-year-old boy was rushed to a hospital suffering from severe burns. The BBC reported on September 29, 2007, that detectives investigating the case said they did not know if the boy had set himself on fire or if it was the result of an attack.

An Unstable Relationship

A Scottish transsexual called 999 screaming "I'm being murdered" and then said something about a "little horse." The caller, Kaye Campbell, didn't have a case of laryngitis; she was referring to a Shetland pony Kaye and her wife, Joanne, kept in their bathroom.

Kaye was cleaning up hoof prints in the bathroom when Joanne went on a rampage about their little pony, threw a knife at Kaye, seized her hair, repeatedly hit her head against a fireplace, and struck her with a flowerpot stand. According to a December 12, 2002, article in the *Daily Record,* Kaye quickly hoofed it out of their home after Joanne's unstable attack. When questioned, Joanne, not wanting to be saddled with charges of aggressive horseplay, denied everything.

No Smoking—
Gas Present

According to a March 22, 2007, story in the Scottish newspaper
Dunfermline Press, Stewart Laidlaw, thirty-five, was banished from
Thirsty Kirsty's pub in the Royal Burgh of Dunfermline, in the town
of Fife, Scotland, after several customers complained about his
noxious emissions. A stunned Laidlaw said no one had complained
about his flatulence before but did state that a new law could be to
blame. On March 26, 2006, Scotland enacted one of the toughest
smoking bans in Europe and now, Laidlaw conceded, there's no
tobacco fumes to cover up the smell.

"THE *DAILY EXPRESS* DECLARES
THAT BRITAIN WILL NOT BE
INVOLVED IN A EUROPEAN WAR THIS
YEAR, OR NEXT YEAR EITHER"

❃ *Daily Express* headline, September 30, 1938 ❃

Not Really a Handy Man

In October 2002, Keith Sanderson, a machine operator at a worktop factory near Newcastle in northeastern England, lost part of his right thumb in a workplace accident. Five months later, on March 19, 2003, Sanderson wanted to show his boss how the accident occurred and replicated the event almost exactly—except this time he cut off a piece of a finger on his left hand.

An Eggstraordinary Story

Images of the Virgin Mary on a grilled cheese sandwich, Jesus on a refrigerator door, Mother Teresa on a cinnamon bun—these all seem like laughable bits of weird news, but what if Christ prophesized his return on freshly laid chicken eggs?

That's just what happened in a small village near Leeds in 1806, when a hen laid an egg with the words "Christ Is Coming" inscribed in black on its shell. Mary Bateman, the hen's owner, announced that God had arrived in a vision to tell her the hen would lay fourteen prophetic eggs; the fourteenth one would usher in the apocalyptic destruction of the world.

But the news wasn't all hard-boiled; God had also bestowed upon Bateman special slips of paper with the inscription "J.C." that were basically "Get into Heaven Free" passes, available for one shilling apiece. More than one thousand people purchased the slips of paper and rested comfortably in the knowledge that they were guaranteed salvation while everyone else was going to burn in hell. A doctor, skeptical of the eggs—or not in on the yoke—examined the eggs and discovered that God had used corrosive ink to write on the shells. He told the local authorities, and they burst into the tavern where the chicken was caged and caught Mary Bateman red-handed shoving the fourteenth inscribed egg into the hen to "lay" later that day.

Bateman was eventually hanged—not for egging people into believing her story but because she later became an abortionist, which was illegal in the nineteenth century.

Tough and Ruthless—
Rough and Toothless

Jason Morris was accused of the vicious crime of taking a pair of pliers and yanking out eighteen of his girlfriend's teeth, leaving her in agonizing pain and covered in her own blood. According to a November 23, 2002, article in the *Guardian,* during the trial in Greater Manchester, the jury acquitted Morris of all charges after his girlfriend, Samantha Court, confessed to extracting the teeth herself.

During Court's day in court she admitted she had pulled her own teeth during a drug binge in an attempt to get rid of a hallucinated green and pink fly that had flown down her throat. Court confided to the jury that, after her dental debacle, she and Morris had decided to stop doing drugs.

Cabin Fever

David Mason was on an SAS Braathens airline flight home to England from Norway when he started thumbing through a pornographic magazine he had brought aboard. When he came to a picture of a black man with a white woman, Mason became outraged and demanded the flight attendant burn the magazine in the plane's galley oven.

According to a September 21, 2004, BBC News report, the stewardess denied Mason's request and sent him back to his seat. A few moments later passengers complained of a burning smell. Mason had set fire to the magazine himself. The crew quickly extinguished the fire, and Mason was arrested when the plane landed.

Charles JJ (1630–85) was noted to have rubbed mummy dust into his skin in order to absorb the greatness of the Egyptian Pharaohs.

Bridging the Gap

Neville Kan, a dentist in Chiswick, England, was acquitted of professional misconduct after being accused of drilling a hole in a patient's tooth and refusing to fill it until the patient paid the £35 she still owed. According to a July 18, 2003, article in the *Daily Telegraph,* the victim, identified as Mrs. B, claimed Kan told her, "Nothing lasts forever, I am not going to last forever. . . . Nothing in life is free. You owe me money." Even if the dentist was acquitted he'll never receive a plaque for that kind of behavior.

Shovel or Nothing

The expression "I can dig it" took on a whole (or hole) new meaning in 2001 when William Lyttle was discovered to have been obsessively digging tunnels underneath his twenty-room house in North London. Lyttle burrowed past his property line, and a cave-in caused a fifteen-foot hole to open up in the street.

Five years later, Lyttle, then in his midseventies, was temporarily removed from his house when it was found that his mole mania had threatened the integrity of the entire street. Because of the holes—combined with the overwhelming amount of junk he had accumulated—his house was in danger of sinking into the ground.

Another Series of Unfortunate Events

The April 13, 2005, edition of the *Telegraph* tells of a bizarre fatal automobile accident involving Alison Taylor and her Peugeot. The Peugeot wouldn't start, so Taylor pulled out a hammer to tap on the starter, as it obviously had a dead spot and wouldn't turn over. She had done this before, but this time she left the keys in the ignition.

When the starter engaged, the car sprang to life, and, as she had also left the car in gear, it began rolling over her. As a reflex she instinctively grabbed something—unfortunately, it was the throttle cable. The car accelerated, dragging Taylor with it, and eventually went over an embankment. The coroner in North Tyneside declared the cause of Taylor's death an accident.

It is still illegal to enter the Houses of Parliament wearing a suit of armor.

A Real General Grievous

Mark Webb, twenty, and Shelley Mandiville, seventeen, of Hemel Hempstead, Hertfordshire, wanted to re-create the lightsaber fight scene from the *Star Wars* film *Revenge of the Sith*. But since neither of them had the Lucas style budget they decided to improvise and took two fluorescent light tubes, filled them with gasoline and dishwashing liquid, and then it was "lights, camera, disaster."

The tubes exploded, covering the two with the flaming mixture. According to a June 23, 2005, article in the *Sun,* police found a video camera next to a badly burned area of ground and suspect that someone was filming the stunt but ran when the two stars became two supernovas.

Nothing on the Ball

In a May 24, 1997, article in *New Scientist,* British scientist David Gems of London's University College provided evidence that males might live longer than females if it weren't for their intense sex drives. He studied normal male marsupial mice who "spend 5 to 11 hours a day copulating" and die after only a few weeks and compared them with castrated marsupial mice who can live for years.

In terms of humans, Gems cited a 1969 study of 319 castrated males (eunuchs) who lived an average of 13.5 years longer than comparable males who still had their testicles. It might be true that castrated men live longer than normal men—but why would they want to?

The Seal of Approval

The Magna Carta, one of the most famous documents in history, created the basis for the writ of habeas corpus, allowing appeal against unlawful imprisonment, and was signed by King John in 1215. Well, almost. The document did proclaim certain rights pertaining to freemen, but the king never signed it—no one ever signed it.

The king, following common law, attached a single seal to the document (which, in order to authenticate the document, had to be done in front of witnesses), but he never signed it—nor did the barons sign the document or even attach their seals to it.

A Cold Reception

Two mental health workers in London who paid a home visit to a woman suffering from paranoid schizophrenia got annoyed because the woman refused to speak to them. In fact, she sat with her back to the two health workers and never answered any of their questions or acknowledged that they were even there. "She didn't seem to want us there," said one health worker.

The following day, two other health workers paid a follow-up visit to the woman and immediately found out why she had given the other two a cold shoulder—she was dead.

"OFFICIAL STATISTICS SAY DON'T TRUST OFFICIAL STATISTICS"

❖ *Lancashire Evening Post* headline, March 18, 2008 ❖

No Joking Matter

A lot of actors take out insurance policies to protect them from fanatic fans, accidents, and loss of whatever they're known for (nice legs, a pug nose, and so forth). But one group of actors decided to take out an insurance policy in case they got sued. The organization, Clowns International, recommended that its members take out "custard pie insurance" in case they are ever sued for hurting someone when they toss a pie.

A spokesclown for the organization said its members should be protected because of "an increasingly litigation-crazy public," not to mention "the ethics and legal implications of 'splatting' and 'sloshing.'" Clown Bluey said, "Clowning is a serious business. If I was a businessman in my best suit I wouldn't appreciate someone coming over and throwing a load of gunge at me."

Bonzo the (Almost) Famous Clown, from East London, said, "If you do throw something at a person they have every right to throw it back. It's all quite harmless really." Martin "Zippo" Burton from Southampton, honorary vice president of Clowns International, admitted that to date no clown has been sued but since a lot of people can't take a joke, it's only a matter of time before the courts see a case named "John Q. Public versus Slappy the Clown."

A Big Flop

Most people have been party to horseplay at work, but one employee at a meatpacking plant in Beccles, Suffolk, in eastern England, obviously got carried away. As three men held down a 10-stone (140-pound) employee, a coworker nicknamed "Honey Monster," who weighed 23 stone (322 pounds), performed a belly flop on the restrained man. The resulting prank left the man with several cracked ribs. A judge ordered Honey Monster to perform 180 hours of community service and awarded the injured man £610. Compared to this, getting popped with a rubber band isn't so bad.

Beer Goggles

Conducting research on alcohol's effect on perception, Barry Jones, a psychology professor at the University of Glasgow, discovered, oddly enough, that after three beers both men and women found members of the opposite sex more attractive. The study, reported in an August 19, 2002, Reuters article, revealed that there was a 25 percent increase in perceived attractiveness after the beers than before them.

Seventy-seven-year-old Maurice Fox told the BBC News on December 4, 2007, that he would comply with the wishes of the Kirkham Street Sports and Social Club of Paignton, Devon, to sit exclusively by the front door so he could quickly exit the establishment when he needed to break wind, of which the management said other patrons had complained.

Don't Get Your Nose Out of Joint

The police department in Northumbria agreed to pay, as workers' compensation, "several thousand dollars" to a detective who now suffers from chronic snoring. The detective, who originally asked for £15,250, claimed the years he spent in the evidence room inhaling dust from seized marijuana plants caused him to have a whistling in his nose and severe snoring, leading to marital disharmony. It also caused a fifteen-year contact high.

Animal Sounds

"Music hath charms to soothe the savage beast" gives the impression that if you played a violin for a charging bull it would stop in its tracks and softly sway to the music. I wouldn't suggest doing that because the above-mentioned statement is misquoted.

What British playwright William Congreve actually says in his play *The Mourning Bride* (1697) is "Music has charms to soothe a savage breast."

A court in Preston, Lancashire,
convicted Akinwale Arobieke
in November 2007 of violating a
2006 court order that forbade him
from accosting men in public and
fondling their biceps.

What Would Dr. Zaius Do?

Most people have had a lousy job at one time in their career—you might be having yours now. But a group of zookeepers in Dudley, West Midlands, could claim one of the smelliest jobs around once a local supermarket donated an enormous batch of Brussels sprouts to the zoo—and the orangutans developed a taste for them.

"Orangutans are windy animals, but because of all the Brussels sprouts they are eating there is quite a pong around here at the moment," said monkey keeper James Harper. He added, "Whoever gets the short straw gets to muck them out." So tell me why, when we were kids, our parents wanted us to eat Brussels sprouts?

Break Like the Wind

In an August 3, 1995, article in the *Edmonton Journal,* Colin Leakey, a respected British scientist, complained that his research has been woefully underfunded. He is looking into the causes of flatulence.

In England, it is against the law for a bed
to be hung out of a window.

Live from the Pasta Farms, This Has Been Al Dente

On April 1, 1957, the BBC aired a documentary on its news show *Panorama* about spaghetti growing in Switzerland. The joke broadcast showed Swiss spaghetti farmers picking fresh spaghetti from "spaghetti trees" and preparing them for market. It also mentioned that the pasta farmers had a bumper crop, partly because of the "virtual disappearance of the spaghetti weevil."

Soon after the broadcast, the BBC received phone calls from viewers eager to know if spaghetti really grew on trees and how they might go about growing a spaghetti tree of their own. To this last question the BBC reportedly replied they should "place a sprig of spaghetti in a tin of tomato sauce and hope for the best."

Getting a Head in Business

According to a "work-love balance" survey conducted in London, nearly two-thirds of employees said they had "enjoyed physical intimacy" in their workplaces, with favorite places being the elevator and the stairwell. The results of the 1,072-worker survey showed that the nasty nurse and dirty doctor stereotype was false, because medical workers are the least likely to indulge in workplace romances. So who are most at risk for "working overtime?" Workers in the leisure and tourism industry, where eight out of ten employees have "pulled an all-nighter."

Bus-ted

Perhaps he was unclear about the concept, couldn't read, or was just overzealous in his job, but a parking warden in Manchester gave a bus driver who had stopped to pick up passengers at a space marked "Buses Only" a ticket for parking at a bus stop.

"All my passengers queuing to get on were gob smacked when the warden dashed over," remembered the bus driver. "He said the area was restricted. When I asked restricted to who, he replied 'buses.' I thought he must be blind." After a complaint to the local council the warden was required to be "retrained." Maybe the man was dyslexic and he thought the bus was at a sub stop.

A Grain of Truth

What does "sow wild oats" mean? Okay, we know the phrase means to commit youthfully foolish acts, but what does that have to do with sowing (not sewing) wild oats?

During the eleventh century, many farmers and peasants left their farms to fight against a multitude of armies who were perpetually invading England. With the farms unattended, many of the domesticated grains reverted to their wild strains. When the warring ceased, a lot of the younger men were eager to settle down and, with no experience in farming, began collecting and planting the seeds from the wild strains of oats. The plants produced were basically useless as they grew very few "heads," which contain the edible seeds. Therefore, it was foolish of these inexperienced young men to waste their time sowing wild oats.

Here Now, the News

King George V (George Frederick Ernest Albert, 1865–1936) reigned from 1910 through 1936. George's health took a bad turn during World War I (1914–18), and the fact that he was a heavy smoker didn't help—he was plagued with emphysema, bronchitis, pleurisy, and other breathing problems.

He fell seriously ill in 1928 and things got progressively worse until, in 1936, he became comatose. His physician, Lord Dawson of Penn, issued a bulletin with words that have become famous: "The King's life is drawing peacefully to a close." Dawson's diary reveals that he administered a lethal injection of cocaine and morphine on the night of January 20, 1936, to ease the strain on the king's family and so that his death could be announced in the morning edition of the *Times*.

Things That Go Bump in the Night

A middle-aged woman in England was awakened by a strange noise in her house and immediately called the police. The bobbies arrived promptly and scoured the residence, looking for the source of the sound. The woman's face went from "white with fear" to "red with embarrassment" when the police discovered that an intruder of another sort had caused the noise: the woman's sex toy vibrating in her nightstand drawer.

A spokesperson for the police said the officers on call had a difficult time keeping a straight face when they apprehended the apparatus. I suppose the term "assault and battery" would apply here—for her next assault she'll need new batteries.

The Lancashire police
concluded their investigation
of Constable Jayson Lobo, finding
him innocent of expense account
misappropriation and ruling
that he had merely committed
errors totalling less than £122. The
Times reported on September 29,
2007, that the investigation cost
the department, and therefore
taxpayers, approximately £610,000.

I Smell a Rat

A postman from London filed for divorce because his wife of thirty-four years continually insisted they share their bed with two others. The woman, a care worker, isn't demanding that she and her husband engage in a *ménage à quatre;* she just refuses to sleep without her two pet ferrets.

The husband complained that the robust-smelling rodents were a nuisance in bed and that his wife spent more time with them than she did with him. He filed on the grounds of unreasonable behavior. Maybe the husband should ferret out the real source of his wife's passive-aggressive behavior before he weasels out of their marriage.

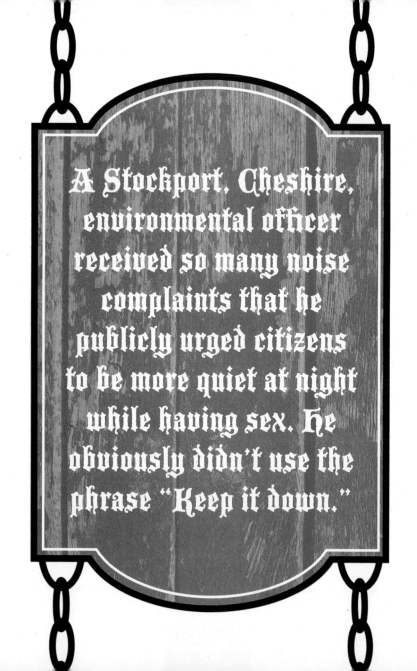

A Stockport, Cheshire, environmental officer received so many noise complaints that he publicly urged citizens to be more quiet at night while having sex. He obviously didn't use the phrase "Keep it down."

The Bride Wore Black

An undertaker, Margaret Cullen, wore a gothic black dress as she walked down the aisle at Strone Church in Dunoon in Argyll, Scotland. She arrived in a hearse for the occasion, but the occasion wasn't a funeral—it was her wedding.

"Undertaking provided us with a great deal of satisfaction and that is why we chose to have a funeral theme" she told the *Daily Record.* The theme included a coffin-shaped wedding cake. The groom in this ghoulish get-together was former undertaker Carl Evans.

"A lot of our guests are also connected with funerals, and I think they appreciated the gesture we made," said the macabre Mrs. Evans. I wonder if the preacher became confused during the "until death do you part" line.

Sooner or Later

A couple from Cliftonville, Kent, spent two years and thousands of dollars planning a round-the-world trip for their twenty-fifth wedding anniversary. Barry and Carol Watson had such a multitude of information to coordinate that it's understandable that they might overlook one insignificant detail—and they did.

The detail they got wrong was the date; they scheduled everything a year too early. While on their twenty-fourth anniversary round-the-world trip, they were too embarrassed to tell their hosts their mistake—but not too embarrassed to give back all the gifts later.

Everyone Got Scrooged

Two days before Christmas 2003, a wife and mother of two, Kim Russell, decided to leave her family for another man. She had been carrying on an Internet romance with the man, and they agreed to finally meet. She entered the hotel room in Yeovil, Somerset, and was so nervous about what she was about to do—and maybe about what she had done to her family—that she died on the spot. An inquest could find no physical reason for the thirty-five-year-old woman's death and in July 2004 ruled it "sudden death syndrome."

"PSYCHIC'S CRYSTAL BALL BURNS DOWN HIS FLAT IN UNFORESEEN BLAZE"

❁ *Times* headline, August 12, 2005 ❁

For Better or Worse

Sharon Carr and Robbie Layne, both serving life sentences for murder, in Broadmoor Prison, called off their wedding after reading a newspaper article about their evil pasts. At twelve years old, Carr was labeled "the devil's daughter" during her trial in 1997 for the brutal stabbing murder of eighteen-year-old Katie Rackliff. The groom-to-be had beaten and stabbed his mother to death and then gouged her eyes out because he thought she was giving his sister more attention. "Obviously they didn't tell each other about their pasts," said a nurse at the Berkshire top-security hospital where they met.

Not Worth Their Metal

At their court appearance for stealing high-tech gas turbine components, the thieves were told that the parts were valued at £4.27 million and could have been the biggest heist ever in Hampshire. The thieves, however, not knowing the true value, had melted everything down and sold it for £915 as scrap metal.

According to a September 13, 2007, article in the *Daily Mail,* police in Hertfordshire resisted criticism for their new program of posting signs reading "Don't Commit Crime." They also installed posters at petrol stations reading "All Fuel Must Be Paid For."

A Fork in the Road

"It's most likely a mix-up with the bar codes," offered the manager of an Asda chain store in Halifax, West Yorkshire. A shopper who was attempting to purchase plates, picnic ware, and teaspoons was asked by the clerk to show proof that she was at least eighteen years old. "Why?" asked the shopper. According to a May 5, 2009, article in the *Telegraph,* the clerk informed the woman that a murder had recently been committed using a teaspoon and now identification was required.

He Said, She Said

Richard Ward claimed he was ordered to get off a United Airlines flight and change clothes before he could continue with his connecting flight home to London. Ward showed United staff his British passport, but they said he wouldn't be allowed to fly until he looked more like the photo on it. What was the problem? Ward was dressed as a woman. Ward, also known as Sarah West, is a transsexual—he even had a letter from his doctor proving it. Ward filed a lawsuit against the airlines in August 2001 for £30,500, and it doesn't look like they'll be able to skirt it.

Driven to the Limit

A British woman who was driving to Calais, in northern France, to run an errand in May 2001 got lost en route. The woman claimed she couldn't find a place to turn around and eventually wound up driving 8,050 kilometers (5,000 miles) through Europe. The unidentified woman drove through France, across the Pyrenees (the mountain range between France and Spain), across Spain, and into Gibraltar. During the extended excursion, she camped out at night with equipment that was fortunately stored in the car. She was finally rescued by her boyfriend and returned home.

"DOH! MAN STEALS GPS TRACKING DEVICE"

❖ *Register* headline, September 4, 2003 ❖

What Happens in Las Vegas . . .

On the night before leaving from his vacation in Las Vegas, Nevada, twenty-one-year-old James Cripps, in a drunken stupor, married a complete stranger from Australia. "If you go to Las Vegas, you drink, you gamble, and you get married," Cripps said. "Which is what I did."

The *Times* reported in November 2001 that Cripps admitted he was "too drunk to consummate" the marriage, but the worst part was telling his girlfriend back home in Bristol, Avon. Cripps said Abi Harding, his girlfriend, "dumped him," though the "exact nature of [her] reaction goes unrecorded."

This Jelly Tastes Weird

Stephen Britland at the University of Bradford and his colleagues, using layers of cells that mimic skin, discovered that "wounds" healed faster after they applied extracts of maggot juice to them. *New Scientist* reported on Britland's experiments on October 9, 2006, and noted that the team had already created a prototype maggot jelly that works just as effectively as directly applying live maggots.

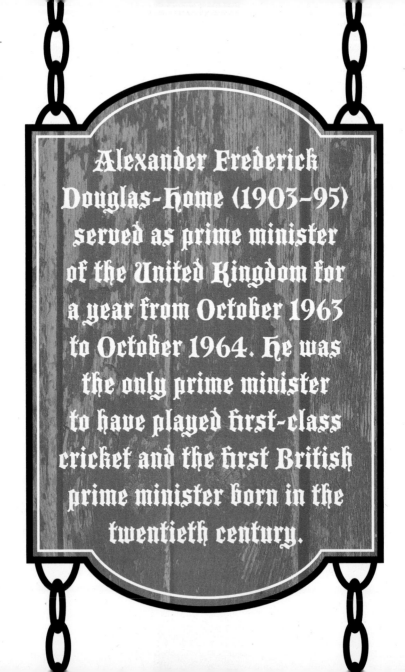

Alexander Frederick Douglas-Home (1903–95) served as prime minister of the United Kingdom for a year from October 1963 to October 1964. He was the only prime minister to have played first-class cricket and the first British prime minister born in the twentieth century.

A Real Rat Race

"You can just imagine a nice, sunny day on Cleveleys Prom, eating your chips, and then this thing goes whizzing past," said a Cleveleys, Lancashire, police officer. He was referring to complaints by vacationers that they were forced to run for cover when they saw a hamster in a race car barreling down the promenade. The hamster, nicknamed Speedy, was apprehended in a toy racing car, powered by a hamster wheel in the middle, and handed over to an animal sanctuary.

Jack Frost Nipped at More Than His Nose

Britain's heat wave in August 2003 claimed dozens of sunburn and heat exhaustion victims, but one man, traveling from London to Manchester, suffered a case of frostbite. "It was incredibly hot," Mike Ball, forty-six, told the *Guardian*. "I slipped off my shoe and sock because my car is an automatic, and I don't need to use my left foot." Ball kept his toes too close to the air-conditioning vent on the 400-kilometer (248-mile) journey and was treated for mild frostbite.

Alan Leigh-Brown of Taunton, Somerset, purchased a DVD copy of the 1957 Doris Day movie *The Pajama Game* to watch with his wife and was shocked to see instead the Italian film *Tettone, che Passione* (Big Tits, What a Passion). According to Leigh-Brown, the couple was so "horrified" and "shocked" that they felt obligated to watch the entire film before returning it.

Citizen Cane

In the 1700s a British gentleman had to buy a license for the privilege of carrying a walking stick and had to abide by a series of strict rules. In order to get a license, he had to agree not to gesture with or wave the walking stick in the air, hang it from his clothing, or tuck it under his arm. Very few gentlemen disregarded these rules, and there was never a cane mutiny.

There really was a King Macbeth. He was the king of Scotland from 1040 to 1057 and his real name was Mac Bethad mac Findlaích (MacBheatha mac Fhionnlaigh in modern Gaelic), which is anglicized as Macbeth, and nicknamed Rí Deircc, "the Red King." He bears little resemblance to the king immortalized in William Shakespeare's tragedy *Macbeth,* however.

The Follicle Follies

A British motorist was cruising down the M6 motorway letting his long hair flap in the breeze when it started to rain. He pressed the button to close the electric sunroof and immediately had a hair-raising experience—his hair was caught and he was being pulled out of the driver's seat.

The bad news is that the man was yanked away from the steering wheel and lost control of the car, which was careening down the motorway at 115 kph (70 mph). The good news is that the man was also pulled away from the accelerator, and the car eventually drifted to a stop in the middle of the motorway.

This Message Will Self-Destruct . . .

During a British Airways flight from London to Los Angeles in June 1999, four hundred passengers were terrified to hear a prerecorded emergency-warning message that was played accidentally. The captain had learned how to respond quickly, however, because this was the third month in a row that an emergency message had accidentally been broadcast into the cabin. In April, the first time the problem arose, a message told passengers the plane was about to crash-land into the Atlantic Ocean.

Because They Don't Know the Words

Tesco, Britain's largest retailer, published an advertisement in the *Sun* announcing their newest product—the whistling carrot. The genetically modified carrot, the ad explained, was specially engineered to grow with air holes along its side that act like little whistles. When placed in a steamer or in a pot to boil, the carrot will whistle like a teakettle to let the cook know it is done.

If this were true it would be great to use on a snowman to make it seem like he's got a clogged nose.

Gary Edwards of Gobowen, Shropshire, proposed to his girlfriend, Jeanette Wilson, in line at a fish and chips shop. Having thought of proposing on the spur of the moment, Edwards didn't have an engagement ring—but he did have an onion ring, which he slipped on her finger. Jeanette told the *Sun,* "I hope he doesn't want to wed me in the local curry house."

Toast and Then Toasted

Two burglars broke into the Kuehne and Nagel Drinks Logistics depot in Swansea, Wales, stacked up about £707 in liquor outside, and then went back in the depot to have a celebratory drink. According to a July 28, 2009, BBC News report, the two boozy burglars got so inebriated that they fell asleep and were discovered the next morning and arrested.

At their hearing, Keith Cullen showed up so drunk he wasn't allowed to enter the building while Paul Wiggins, who was allowed in, disappeared before the hearing started. Both men were tried in absentia and convicted of burglary and theft.

Hooligans Win!

The *Irish Times* reported in February 1992 about a recently won lawsuit filed by thirty-eight Irish soccer fans against two independent Italian bus companies. The lawsuit claimed that the bus drivers were at fault for making them miss the 1990 World Cup games in Italy. They testified that the bus drivers purposely drove inordinately slow (averaging only 32 kph—or 20 mph) on two trips, making the fans miss one game and then later miss the ferry that would have taken them to another game.

"BRITISH DUCKS HAVE REGIONAL ACCENTS, RESEARCHERS SAY"

❀ BBC News headline, June 4, 2004 ❀

What About Rocket Scientists, Then?

The *Daily Telegraph* reported on September 2, 2003, that Britain's Donald Campbell had crashed his twin-engine plane into a house after it had run out of fuel. The article explained that Campbell, who suffered head injuries as a result of the accident, had miscalculated the amount of fuel when he attempted to convert gallons to liters. This gives a new twist to an old saying, as Mr. Campbell is, in fact, a brain surgeon.

Do I Make You Horny?

London's High Court approved an insurance settlement in March 2007 for £1.465 million for motorcyclist Kunal Lindsay, who was struck by an automobile in 2002. After extensive physical therapy, Lindsay noted that he had become uncontrollably and chronically horny and had acquired an unhealthy attraction to cell phones. The *Daily Telegraph* reported on March 2, 2007, that the court was convinced that the accident had caused these conditions, which, because of Lindsay's constant nagging of his wife for sex, led to the breakup of Lindsay's marriage.

A member of the House of Lords, Norman Tebbit, told a radio interviewer that homosexuality in Britain is "intimately connected" to the rise in obesity. He explained that homosexuality is causing a breakdown of the traditional family, which means fewer family meals and more fattening fast food.

Droning On

According to his mother, when David Armour of Glasgow was thirteen years old, he "wheezed all the time and could not do any exercise," because of his severe asthma. The *Daily Record* reported on July 7, 2007, that after two years Armour had a complete recovery. It was attributed not to medical treatments, but to the fact that he had been diligently learning to play the bagpipes.

According to an April 13, 2007, article in the *Daily Mail,* Andrew Workman accidentally crashed his car into another in Shepley, West Yorkshire, after he lost control when a bee flew through the window and stung him in the crotch.

Gee, You Are You

The popular '60s singer Donovan (born Donovan Leitch in the Maryhill area of Glasgow), announced in October 2007 that he plans, along with director David Lynch, to open the Invincible Donovan University in Edinburgh. Donovan explained that his guru in the '60s told him to build a university to advance Transcendental Meditation teachings and that Donovan is prepared to finally follow through with that request.

"For a country the size of Scotland it would take only 250 students meditating to protect Scotland from its enemies and to bring peace, to stop violence and drug abuse," Lynch said. "That is just a byproduct of the students meditating together."

What's the Buzz About?

New Scientist magazine reported on September 9, 2004, about a team of British scientists who are developing a robot that will produce its own electric power by eating flies. The power system of the EcoBot II (short for Ecological Robot) was created to break down the sugar in the flies' bodies by digesting it in specially designed fuel cells—converting the sugar into electrons. While an energetically autonomous robot is a breakthrough, there is a drawback: In order to attract the flies needed to power the robot it will have to be smeared with sewage or excrement.

"DEFENDANT STOLE BICYCLE TO GET TO COURT ON TIME"

❧ *Guardian* headline, June 13, 2006 ❧

Keeping an Eye Out

In 1801, Captain Horatio Nelson,of the British navy was engaged in attacking French troops in Copenhagen, Denmark. The tide of the battle turned in favor of the French, and Nelson was ordered by the command ship to retreat. But Nelson wanted to continue fighting and ignored the command. A subordinate urged the captain to heed the commander's order, and Nelson picked up a telescope to verify the signal for himself. But Nelson, who was blind in one eye, purposely put the telescope up to his sightless eye and said truthfully that he couldn't see any signal of retreat. Nelson continued his attack and won. This event left us with a phrase that means to ignore something: to turn a blind eye.

Family Reunion

David Norris's father left home when he was five months old, and he never saw him again. Norris turned to a life of crime and is serving a minimum twelve-year sentence for murder and rape and is housed in Peterhead Prison. According to an August 26, 2008, article in the Scottish *Daily Record,* soon after arriving at Peterhead, Norris met thirty-nine-year-old David Gilles, serving a life sentence for kidnapping and sexual torture, and realized that Gilles is his father.

The English horn is neither English nor a horn.
Its origins are in the Near East, it was improved and
redeveloped in Vienna, and it is a woodwind.

Because They're Both Small and Annoying

In November 2005, British inventor Howard Stapleton introduced a sound device called the Mosquito that emits an annoying high-frequency sound wave, measuring about 17 KHz, which adolescents up to twenty can hear but which diminishes in their thirties. The device was created to dissuade unruly youths from hanging out in front of businesses while not having any effect on adult shoppers.

Adolescents turned the tide on adults, according to a June 12, 2006, article in the *Times,* by using the technology of the Mosquito and downloading the high-frequency sound as a ring tone in their cell phones. That way they can receive incoming calls and text messages without school officials knowing about it.

It's Hammer Time

While preparing to leave for a fancy dress party to celebrate New Year's Eve 2008, Torvald Alexander came face-to-face with a man who had broken into his apartment. When the bumbling burglar saw Alexander, he turned and hurriedly climbed out of a window, rolled down a sloped roof, slammed into the ground, and took off running. According to a January 2, 2009, BBC News report, the robber apparently was terrified at seeing Alexander who, at the time, was dressed as Thor, the hammer-wielding Norse god of thunder.

He Can't Follow Directions Anyway

Sixteen-year-old Darren Mirren filed an age-discrimination suit against the Spotless Commercial Cleaning Company in Glasgow. The company is located approximately twenty minutes from Mirren's house, but he claimed he was unable to arrive for a job interview and was subsequently rejected for a position. According to an August 26, 2008, article in the *Scotsman,* Mirren implied that because of his young age the company should have been more responsible in giving him directions.

"DRIVER SHOCKED AS SHEEP EMERGES FROM POTHOLE"

Western Mail (Wales), September 23, 2000

Don't Wine About It

According to a November 2, 2007, article in *Der Spiegel,* Catholic priests in Ireland and Northern Ireland expressed concern with their respective governments' proposals to lower the legal blood-alcohol level for driving from .08 to .05. The priests complained that because of a shortage of available priests, they are required to drive greater distances to conduct Masses. And, they reminded authorities, as they are obliged to drink any leftover sacramental wine from every Mass they conduct, there would be the distinct probability that they would exceed the newly enacted blood-alcohol level.

Expressing Yourself

A UK student wrote "F**k off" as his sole submission on his General Certificate of Secondary Education exam. Instead of being punished, the student was given 7.5 percent additional credit because he demonstrated "nominal skills" by turning in any answer as opposed to leaving the page empty. According to a July 1, 2008, article in the *Mirror,* chief examiner Peter Buckroyd said he would have received even more credit if he had used an exclamation point—demonstrating his understanding of punctuation.

Urine Trouble Now

A judge at Killorglin District Court in Kerry, Ireland, agreed with the two defendants' lawyer and dismissed the DUI cases against them because the blood-alcohol readings were not properly administered. Standard procedure calls for people suspected of DUI to be isolated for twenty minutes before the test, but in this case they were allowed to use the restrooms. According to a December 1, 2008, article in the *Belfast Telegraph,* the suspects' lawyer claimed that inhaling the "steam" from their urine could have raised their blood-alcohol readings.

According to a recent survey, Britons spend more than
ninety minutes a day gossiping, e-mailing friends,
and flirting in the office.

Nine Lives

The Life and Adventures of a Cat was a racy and risqué book that was published in England in 1760. The book centered on a ram cat (the name male cats went by back then) named Tom the Cat. The book was so amazingly popular that from that point on male cats have been commonly called "tomcats."

Cat Got Your Tongue?

During the murder trial of seventy-two-year-old David Henton of Swansea, Wales, police testified that they had hidden microphones in Henton's house and recorded him confessing to the killing of his longtime domestic partner. Since Henton lived alone after murdering his partner—to whom was he talking? Apparently, according to a January 16, 2008, BBC News report, Henton frequently held long conversations with his cats, and during one of his diatribes he confessed to the murder.

May the Force Be with You

A judge from Holyhead, Wales, suspended a two-month jail sentence for a man who had attacked two men while wearing a black cape and black trash bag in a drunken attempt to portray *Star Wars* villain Darth Vader. According to an April 22, 2008, BBC News story, Arwel Wynne Hughes attacked Barney Jones, founder of the first British Jedi church, and his cousin with a metal crutch as they were filming themselves fighting with "lightsabers." Hughes's lawyer asked for leniency, as his client was an alcoholic and was seeking treatment for his addiction.

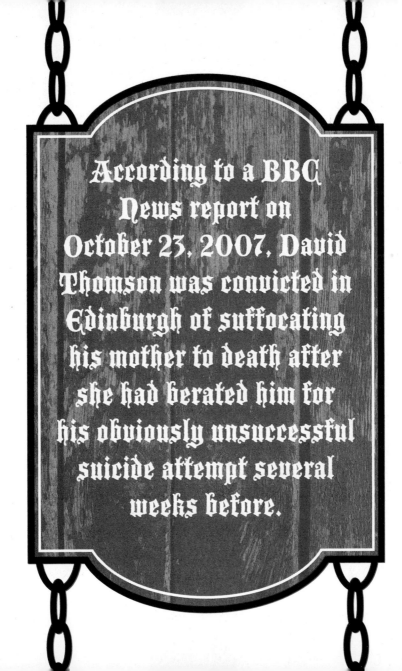

According to a BBC News report on October 23, 2007, David Thomson was convicted in Edinburgh of suffocating his mother to death after she had berated him for his obviously unsuccessful suicide attempt several weeks before.

Van Go

"I was on my way to a shop to buy some tea bags when the council official pulled me over [and issued me a fixed penalty notice for smoking in a workplace]," Gordon Williams of Llanafan, Wales, complained. The main reason Williams was upset was that he wasn't in a workplace—he was in his privately owned van. Williams, a self-employed decorator, told the *Telegraph* on July 25, 2008, that he plans to fight the fine in court because "[My van is] not my place of work. I decorate houses, not vans."

Up, Up, and Away

Lefkos Hajji of Hackney, London, wasn't just full of hot air when he stated that he had come up with a unique way to propose to his girlfriend. He inserted his fiancé's £6,000 ring into a balloon and filled it with helium so she could prick it with a pin and he could literally "pop the question."

But when he took the bunch of balloons outside, a sudden gust of wind pulled them from his hands, and he watched helplessly as they soared into the sky. "I felt like such a plonker," he told the *London Telegraph* on March 14, 2008. Hajji's fiancé, Leanne, almost popped when she heard the news and has demanded a new ring with no strings attached.

Was This His Finest Hour?

In March 2008, a survey commissioned by Walt Disney Studios Home Entertainment and the Royal Astronomical Society found that a third of Britain's children ages four to ten thought that Sir Winston Churchill was the first man to set foot on the moon. "It's a bit of a worry to find that children don't know who the first man on the moon is, let alone that they don't know who led the country to victory in the Second World War," said Gavin Quirk, a Disney brand manager.

An archaic law requiring London taxi drivers to carry a bale of hay on top of their cabs to feed their horses wasn't repealed until 1976.

This Is My
Good Friend Harvey

In 1726, an English maid, Mary Toft, reported to the authorities that she had been accosted and molested by a six-foot rabbit. Some of the townsfolk were skeptical, but some actually believed her and ordered their wives and daughters to stay inside at night and, of course, not to open the door to any six-foot rabbits.

Five months after the rabbit rape, Mary collapsed in a field and was declared pregnant by a local doctor. A little over a month later, Mary gave birth and the baby looked just like its father—a rabbit. Over the next few days Mary gave birth to seven more rabbits, all of them dead. News of the bunny babies reached King George I, and he sent two of England's finest physicians to investigate.

The doctors performed various tests on the dead rabbits and amazingly declared that the births were genuine. Under the direction of a third expert, Mary was moved to a London hospital and put under round-the-clock surveillance. During that time Mary didn't move a hare.

A gardener eventually confessed he had been supplying Mary and her husband with baby rabbits, and Mary finally admitted to the ruse. She told authorities the motivation behind the hoax was that her husband had lost his job and they were hoping for a pension from the king. The king did give Mary something—a prison term for fraud. I guess the king was angry about the deception; you could say he was hopping mad.

A Different Kind of Cheese Roll

The Cooper's Hill Cheese Rolling and Wake is an annual event that has been held for the last two hundred years on the Spring Bank Holiday at Cooper's Hill, near Gloucester. It used to be a local event for the citizens of the village of Brockworth, but now thousands of people show up to take part in the tradition. And what is the tradition, you might ask? A large wheel of Double Gloucester cheese is rolled down a dangerously steep hill while hundreds of people race, fall, and roll down after it. The first to the bottom gets the cheese.

During World War JJ cheese was rationed, so from 1941 to 1954 a wooden "cheese" was used instead. A small piece of real cheese was inserted into a hollow space in the wooden replica.

Quicker Than a Grindstone

At the beginning of the Victorian era in Great Britain, Thomas Saverland approached Caroline Newton in a jocular fashion and attempted to kiss her. She rejected his advances and then chewed him out—well, actually she just chewed off a piece of his nose. Saverland took Newton, the nose gnasher, to court in 1837, but she was acquitted. The judge ruled: "When a man kisses a woman against her will she is fully entitled to bite his nose, if she so pleases." I wonder if the judge polled the jury and then counted the "ayes" and the "nose."

The Last Rung

Seventy-three-year-old Anthony Gower-Smith sued the Hampshire County Council after he fell off a six-foot stepladder at a primary school near Romsey, Hampshire, where he worked as a janitor. Gower-Smith admitted in court that over the previous thirty years he had frequently used similar ladders without incident and even marked a box acknowledging he had received "ladder training."

He countered by saying, "When you are given something to sign by your superior you just sign it." Although Gower-Smith told police at the accident site that he had been standing on the top of the ladder and that the accident was his fault, he later claimed, "I don't remember what I said. I was dazed." According to a June 17, 2008, article in the *Sun*, the court thought that that was a good enough reason to judge him only 25 percent at fault. Since he was suing for up to £50,000, he could receive up to £37,500 in damages.

Ask and Ye Shall Receive

As reported in an August 13, 2008, article in the *Lancashire Evening Post,* the English Heritage Society, an organization responsible for maintaining many of the most important sites in the United Kingdom, released a list of some of the unique, strange, and stupid questions visitors have asked them. Among them were:

* "Why did they build so many ruined castles and abbeys in England?"
* "What time do you switch the mist off?" (asked during a misty day at Dover Castle)
* "Can you tell me where I can see the Hobbits?"
* "How long does life membership last?"
* "Are the tunnels underground?" (asked at the secret wartime tunnels in Kent)
* "Is that man-made?" (asked about a three-hundred-million-year-old rock formation)

Holmes Is Where the Heart Is

The fictional detective Sherlock Holmes is known for his deductive reasoning, his calabash pipe, his deerstalker hat, and his catchphrase "Elementary, my dear Watson." But even fictional characters aren't safe from being fictionalized. Case in point, my dear reader: Between 1887 and 1927, Sir Arthur Conan Doyle published four novels and fifty-six short stories about the celebrated detective and his physician-sidekick, Dr. John H. Watson—and not once is a calabash pipe, a deerstalker hat, or the phrase "Elementary, my dear Watson" mentioned. So why are these things attributed to him?

Over the years, actors portraying Sherlock Holmes have embellished his dress and his speech. Side note: Holmes was a Victorian and wouldn't have made the fashion faux pas of wearing a deerstalker hat (country apparel) in the city—and I've just proven I'm a plonker.

Don't Go Changing to Try and Please Me . . .

Alexander Pope, generally regarded as the greatest English poet of the eighteenth century, embarked on a verse translation of Homer's *Iliad,* published in six volumes from June 1715 to May 1720. Charles Montagu, the Earl of Halifax, was a subscriber to Pope's translation and arranged for a reading before the work was published.

Pope wrote about the reading, and Montagu's suggestions: "In four or five places Lord Halifax stopped me very civilly [saying that] there is something in that passage that does not quite please me. Be so good as to mark the place. . . . I'm sure you can give it a better turn." Pope made no change in his text and reread the exact passages to Montagu some time later. The earl gloated that he was entirely satisfied with the corrections.

The Key to Success

Amanda Webster of London called the Royal Automobile Club when she couldn't get her Ford Focus to start during a shopping trip with her one-year-old son, Oscar. According to a December 3, 2002, article in the *Telegraph,* it soon became evident that the problem was that the aspirin-sized coded radio transponder from her car's key was missing. And since little Oscar had been playing with the keys earlier, he was the prime suspect. Mothers are some of the most ingenious people on the planet, and Webster had the brilliant idea of holding Oscar close to the steering wheel and turning the key in the ignition. The car started right up. Mom and baby made a safe journey back home, and eventually the transponder made a safe journey through Oscar's body.

When Walter Met Elizabeth

The scene: Queen Elizabeth I walks down a London street followed by her entourage and stops in front of a puddle of mud. Suddenly Sir Walter Raleigh breaks through the crowd and drapes his cloak over the puddle so the queen can walk on unmuddied. It's a scene that's been duplicated and parodied in theater and films for decades, but one small detail is usually overlooked—it never happened.

This romantic story is the invention of Thomas Fuller, a seventeenth-century historian, who embellished otherwise boring historical stories, or, in this case, made them up altogether. In 1821, Sir Walter Scott elaborated on the falsehood in his novel *Kenilworth* with an exchange between the two famous sixteenth-century personalities: Raleigh says admirably he will never have his cloak cleaned, to which the queen graciously offers him a tailor-made suit for his gallant actions. Very sweet, very poignant, very much made up.

What a Sight

Praising residents for surpassing recycling goals, the Birmingham City Council distributed about 720,000 flyers with "Thank You Birmingham!" written over a picture of the Birmingham skyline. What's so stupid about that? Nothing, until you realize they used the skyline of Birmingham, Alabama, in the United States, not Birmingham, West Midlands. What makes this more embarrassing, according to an August 14, 2008, Associated Press article, is that this is the second time in the same year that Birmingham has used the wrong cityscape to promote itself.

An accident on June 6, 2008, at the Albion Chemicals plant in Belfast, Northern Ireland, caused a cloud of nitric acid to form over parts of the town. A spokesperson for the plant said there was no cause for alarm as the leak was primarily nitrous oxide, commonly known as "laughing gas." A reporter for the Associated Press commented that there was no unusual "giggling" reported in the area.

That's Crazy!

Although it has been called various names throughout its long history—St. Mary Bethlehem, Bethlem Hospital, Bethlehem Hospital, and the Hospital of St. Mary of Bethlehem—it will forever go down in history as Bedlam. The hospital began taking people with mental illnesses in 1357, and it even became a tourist attraction where Londoners could pay a penny to stare and laugh at the antics of the inmates. According to *The Catholic Encyclopedia,* "Visitors were permitted to bring long sticks with which to poke and enrage the inmates." The word "bedlam," meaning uproar or confusion, is derived from the name of this notorious hospital.

The playwright Nathaniel Lee was incarcerated at Bedlam for five years (1684–89), reporting that "They called me mad, and I called them mad, and damn them, they outvoted me."

A Round of Golf

1452: One of the earliest known references to golf is when King James II of Scotland banned play of the game (along with soccer), claiming it interfered with his subjects' archery practice.

1471: King James III of Scotland reaffirms the ban on golf.

1491: King James IV of Scotland reaffirms the ban on golf.

1502: King James IV of Scotland repeals the ban on golf and then takes up the game himself. He also makes the first recorded purchase of golf equipment, a set of clubs from a bow maker in Perth.

In 1592, the laws against golf were modified under King James VI to forbid the sport only on the Sabbath. That law was later softened to outlaw golf only "in tyme of sermons."

Watch Your Tongue

On July 5, 2003, the BBC reported on twenty-six-year-old Becky Nyang, who was on vacation on the Greek island of Corfu when she was struck by lightning. The airport worker from Reading, Berkshire, was left with severe blisters about the mouth, face, and feet (where the lightning exited) after the metal stud in her tongue attracted the lightning.

The Best of the Worst

In February 1997, forty-five-year-old Sue Evans-Jones of Yate, South Gloucestershire, passed her driver's test after three failed attempts. However, Evans-Jones drove away ten instructors during the 1,800 lessons and twenty-seven years she took to learn her driving skills. Most of the instructors had told her she was such a terrible driver that it would be best if she never received a license.

"PIG NOT DEGRADED BY TELEVISED SEXUAL EXPERIENCE, BRITISH WATCHDOG RULES"

Agence France-Presse headline, November 29, 2004

The Cottingley Fairies

In 1917, sixteen-year-old Elsie Wright and her ten-year-old cousin Frances Griffiths not only claimed they'd played with fairies in the garden of their home in Cottingley; they even had photographs to prove it. The pictures caused a sensation around the world and made many people believe in the world of fairies and the occult— Sir Arthur Conan Doyle, creator of Sherlock Holmes, became one of the fairies' most outspoken supporters.

But in 1981, the two women finally admitted that the whole thing had been a hoax and that they had cut pictures of fairies out of a book and attached them to leaves and limbs with paperclips before taking the photographs. "How on earth anyone could be so gullible as to believe that they were real has always been a mystery to me," Frances Griffiths exclaimed in amazement.

Under There— Under Where?

Police in Preesall, Lancashire, arrested their town's mayor, Ian Stafford, on suspicion of stealing women's knickers from various homes in the area. Police launched an investigation after a series of complaints from women who found items of their lingerie missing. According to an August 24, 2009, article in the *Sun,* police uncovered a cache of underwear in Stafford's home. He resigned shortly after his arrest.

It is illegal for a Welshman to enter the city of Chester after dark.

A Crappy Landing

Noel Atkins, the mayor of Worthing, West Sussex, overcame his fear of heights and took part in a parachute jump for charity, according to an August 2, 2009, article in the *Argus*. As Atkins sat in the airplane's doorway he started having second thoughts; was it fear, he wondered, or the greasy bacon sandwich he had for lunch? The jump went according to plan, all except the landing: "It was a very comfy, soft landing," Atkins said. "In the biggest cow pat you can imagine."

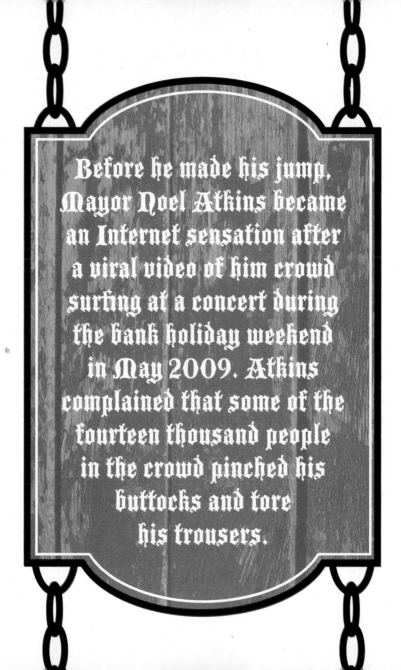

Before he made his jump, Mayor Noel Atkins became an Internet sensation after a viral video of him crowd surfing at a concert during the bank holiday weekend in May 2009. Atkins complained that some of the fourteen thousand people in the crowd pinched his buttocks and tore his trousers.

Scat, You!

According to a June 11, 2007, *Metro* article, Mr. Bonney Eberendu was sentenced to a mental health facility by a judge in London's Southwark Crown Court after Eberendu confessed to smearing his feces inside at least six trains over a period of several months. In his defense, Eberendu said that on at least five occasions, the voices in his head had ordered him to murder somebody—but he was able to override that desire by wiping his poop on things while riding the rails.

Boys Don't Cry

In a May 17, 2003, article, the *London Free Press* told the strange story of battered wife Elizabeth Rudavsky, who was charged with the stabbing death of her severely abusive husband, Angelo Heddington. Rudavsky had been married for seven months but apparently never noticed that Heddington was missing something. Was it compassion? The ability to control himself? No. It was a penis. Heddington wasn't a man at all; she was a woman.

A former girlfriend of Heddington who knew her secret told a reporter, "[Heddington] had soft hands, but she spit like a guy. The whole time you were talking to her, she'd have her hands in her pockets playing with herself like she was a guy."

Down in the Mouth

This story will make you clinch your jaw and other parts of your body. According to a January 13, 2007, article in the *Daily Telegraph,* the British General Dental Council found dentist David Quelch guilty of serious professional misconduct. The council ruled that Quelch could no longer practice dentistry after he pulled two teeth out of an eighty-seven-year-old patient, against her will, without anesthesia, because she had complained about previous treatments. He was quoted as saying, "That'll teach you not to complain."

"FATHER CHRISTMAS WAS PUNCHED IN HIS GROTTO"

❖ *Dorset Echo* headline, December 2, 2008 ❖

Boxer's Boxers

Featherweight boxer Richard Procter thought he was the local favorite after he jumped in the ring at the World Sporting Club in London on July 11, 2004. He tossed off his robe and listened to the thunderous applause from the crowd. It was only then that he realized he had forgotten to put his shorts on.

A man from North Wales called 999 to report a "bright stationary object" in the sky that, he claimed, had remained for over a half hour.

He begged for an officer to be dispatched. According to a July 4, 2008, article in the *Daily Mail,* the police report stated that the object in question was the moon.

Skirting the Issue

The kilt, a traditional Scottish garment, isn't as traditional as one might think. It was actually invented around 1727 by Thomas Rawlinson, an Englishman. Rawlinson owned an ironworks and thought that the real traditional Highland Scots outfit, a plaid knee-length garment belted at the waist, interfered with his employees' efficiency. The garment was cumbersome and looked like a blanket draped around their bodies—in fact, the Gaelic word "plaid" means "blanket."

Rawlinson encouraged his workers to wear his new design by wearing it himself, and soon the fad caught on. Things went so well, in fact, that Parliament banned the kilt in 1745 as a threat to the British way of life. After that, every Scot had to have one in their wardrobe.

Pass the Gravy

And did those feet in ancient time walk upon England's gravy
scene? That's what organizers of the World Gravy Wrestling
Championships hoped for when twenty-four people climbed into a
messy ring of gravy to raise money for charity.

Bisto donated two thousand liters of gravy past its "best before"
date, and the fire brigade stood by to hose down the gravy groupies
gathered at the Rose 'n' Bowl pub in Stacksteads, Lancashire.
The BBC News reported on August 31, 2009, that the men's
competition was won by Joel Hicks, who wrestled under the name
Stone Cold Bisto, while Emma Slater—who was dressed as Mrs.
Christmas—won the women's event.

The New Good Book

The Church of England has published new guidelines in a book called *Everybody Welcome,* urging that worshippers with "special needs" should be more warmly received in church. According to a July 25, 2009, article in the *Telegraph,* the book claims that only one in ten church visitors return because existing worshippers tend to be so unwelcoming.

Those with "special needs," according to the book, are the blind, the deaf, people in wheelchairs, very short people, overweight people ("Some pew spaces and chairs are embarrassingly inadequate for what is known in church circles as 'the wider community,'" the book says), breast-feeding mothers, bald people (who could suffer "trouble from those overhead radiant heaters some churches have unwittingly installed"), and those who read tabloid newspapers.